W9-AJS-986

9 1160 00539 2860

GAMES

LEARN TO PLAY, PLAY TO WIN

DANIEL KING

KINGFISHER
a Houghton Mifflin Company imprint
222 Berkeley Street
Boston, Massachusetts 02116
www.houghtonmifflinbooks.com

Author	**Daniel King**
Illustrators	**Julie Hartigan, Mike Buckley**
Managing Editor	**Russell Mclean**
Deputy Art Director	**Mike Buckley**
Senior Production Controller	**Debbie Otter**
DTP Manager	**Nicky Studdart**
Picture Research Manager	**Cee Weston-Baker**
Indexer	**Hilary Bird**

First published by Kingfisher Publications Plc 2003

1 3 5 7 9 10 8 6 4 2

1TR/0503/TEC/MAR(MAR)/128MA

LIBRARY OF CONGRESS CATALOGING-IN-PUBLICATION DATA
King, Daniel.
Games : learn to play, play to win / by Daniel King.—1st ed.
p. cm.
Includes index.
Summary: Provides instructions on how to play a range of card and board games, as
well as strategy and history of the games.
Contents: Introduction to board games—Ancient board games—Nine men's morris—
Fox and geese—Backgammon—Go—Chess—Mancala—Checkers—Introduction to
card games—Children's card games—Solo card games—Rummy—Cribbage—Whist
—Spades—Hearts—Pontoon—Poker.
1. Board games—Juvenile literature. 2. Card games—Juvenile literature. [1. Board
games. 2. Card games. 3. Games.] I. Title.

GV1312.K53 2003
794—dc21

The web site addresses listed in this book are correct at the time of going to print. However, due to the ever-changing nature of the Internet, web site addresses and content can change. Web sites can contain links that are unsuitable for children. The publisher cannot be held responsible for changes in web site addresses or content, or for information obtained through third-party web sites. We strongly advise that Internet searches should be supervised by an adult.

The publisher would like to thank the following for permission to reproduce their material. Every care has been taken to trace copyright holders. However, if there have been unintentional omissions or failure to trace copyright holders, we apologize and will, if informed, endeavor to make corrections in any future edition.

Key: b = bottom, c = center, l = left, r = right, t = top

4tl Bridgeman / British Museum; 4bl Bridgeman / Czartoryski Museum, Krakow, Poland; 4 Daniel King; 5tl www.chessmaster.com; 5tr Corbis / Margaret Courtney-Clarke; 5br Daniel King; 6tl Bridgeman / Fitzwilliam Museum, University of Cambridge; 6bl Bridgeman / Vatican Museums and Galleries, Vatican City; 6–7 Art Archive; 7tr Art Archive; 7br Bridgeman / Victoria & Albert Museum; 8tr British Museum; 8cl Art Archive / Turin Museum; 8cr Corbis / Mimmo Jodice; 8br AKG / Lobdengau Museum, Landenburg; 9bl Bridgeman / Royal Asiatic Society, London; 9tr National Museum of Ireland, Dublin; 9br Lady PegLeg; 24tl British Museum; 30t British Museum; 31br Kingfisher plc; 38tl Topkapi Museum, Istanbul; 38cl www.wopc.co.uk; 38cb Bridgeman / British Library; 39b Corbis / Bettmann; 40bl Bridgeman / Museo Correr, Venice, Italy; 40–41 Corbis / Angelo Hornak; 41bl Art Archive / Musée Carnavalet Paris / Dagli Orti; 41cr Corbis / Bennett Dean; Eye Ubiquitous; 46 Hulton Getty

If you have any comments about this book, please contact the author: dan@danielking.biz

ISBN 0-7534-5581-1

Printed in China

CONTENTS

BOARD GAMES

CARD GAMES

REFERENCE

▲ *Our ancestors were just as passionate about board games as we are today. This Egyptian board is more than 3,000 years old.*

INTRODUCTION

Games excite, thrill, amuse, and frustrate us. Some people can become so fascinated by a game that they devote their lives to understanding it. Games are a central part of our culture. Every day we use expressions from games—people talk of a political "stalemate" or someone's "checkered" career.

Today we play a wide range of games on computers or on game boards. Most of them are actually versions of much older, highly sophisticated board games that were played by ancient civilizations all over the world.

▶ *In 2002 world chess champion Vladimir Kramnik took on Deep Fritz— the strongest chess computer in the world. The eight-game match was a tie.*

◀ *Trictrac, a version of backgammon, was popular in Europe for around 400 years. This ornate board was made in Poland in 1584.*

MORE THAN A GAME

Throughout the ages games have mostly been played for fun and intellectual stimulation. That is true today, but now games are also played for other reasons. Games are used as teaching aids in schools, and some people even earn money from playing games.

◀ Computer board games have been a major innovation over the last two decades. Playing against a machine can be a great way to improve your game.

◀ Mancala is mostly played in Africa, but it is now recognized around the world as an excellent tool for teaching mathematics.

PROFESSIONAL PLAYERS

Professional games players make their living by competing in tournaments. Whether the game is chess, checkers, or go, important title matches are broadcast all over the world on TV and through the Internet. In Japan the best go players are celebrities. Important matches get extensive coverage all over the Far East.

INTERNET INFLUENCE

The Internet has breathed new life into many ancient games, allowing people from all over the world to play against each other—online and in real time. It has popularized games, such as go and mancala, that were traditionally only played in particular parts of the world.

GAMES FOR LIFE

Games play an important role in education—just like in life, we have to learn to play by certain rules; we cannot undo our actions, but we must learn to accept responsibility; we learn that being creative can lead to success; we learn how to analyze our strategies and our actions and how to improve them for the next time. Games also teach us the hardest lesson of all—how to accept defeat and victory equally.

▼ Dama, or Turkish checkers, is a popular board game throughout the Middle East.

▲ *The ancient Egyptian game of mehen was played on a snake-shaped board. It dates back to 3000 B.C. A version of mehen is still played in Sudan.*

ANCIENT GAMES I

Some board games are so well constructed that we believe they must be the invention of one person. Many myths support this idea. It is said that the Chinese game of go (also known as wei-chi) was invented by the Emperor Yao around 2200 B.C. to strengthen the mind of his mentally disabled son, Shokin.

THE MYTH OF THE FOOLISH KING

Chess is thought to have been invented by a vizier, or adviser, to an Indian king. The king was so impressed by the game that he offered his vizier a reward. The vizier asked for a grain of rice on the first square of the chessboard, two grains of rice on the second square, four grains on the third square, eight on the next square, and so on, doubling the number of grains until each of the 64 squares were filled. The king readily agreed to such a humble reward but soon realized there was not enough rice in the kingdom to satisfy the request. The king had been made to look like a fool, and the vizier was beheaded.

▲ *This wine pitcher from around 540 B.C. shows the ancient Greek heroes Ajax and Achilles in intellectual combat over a board game.*

▶ *These Roman dice and game counters are made of bone. Their design is similar to those we use today for games such as backgammon.*

HOW GAMES REALLY BEGAN

From around 12,000 years ago humans began to live together in communities. They lived in houses, harvested crops, and traded their surplus goods with other villages. They had more security than their ancestors—nomads who wandered the land searching for food—and were able to spend time away from work. Playing games became the perfect way to spend their free time.

FROM RELIGION TO RACING

Archaeologists have found evidence of board games dating back to the earliest civilizations of the Middle East, India, and China. Many games appear to have developed from religious ceremonies in which an early type of die was thrown in order to predict the future. It is easy to imagine how this led to counters being used to keep a record of the scores and how the moving counters could be seen as similar to racing athletes or horses.

These "race games" are the most ancient board games we know about, and they were played by cultures all over the world. They are still the most common type of game—snakes and ladders, ludo, and backgammon all involve racing counters around a board, and all three have ancient beginnings.

▲ Backgammon was very popular in medieval Europe. This illustration is from the famous Book of Games, written in 1282 for Alfonso the Wise, King of Castile (an area in modern-day Spain).

▶ This 19th-century print shows two Japanese go players in heated competition. To be successful at board games, however, it is best to control your emotions and remain calm.

ANCIENT GAMES II

The origins of race games, such as backgammon, probably lie in the ancient cultures of the Middle East. The oldest complete game board was discovered in the royal graves of Ur, an ancient city in Sumer (an area that is now in southern Iraq).

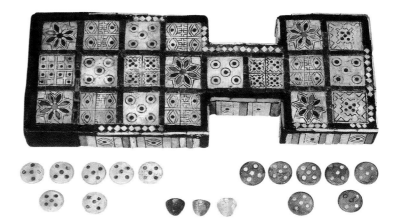

▲ *The royal game of Ur dates back to around 2500 B.C. Each player raced seven counters around the board, and their moves were determined by pyramid-shaped dice. The game was probably played in the Middle East for more than 2,000 years. Boards have been found scratched into temple floors from a much later period, and the rules were discovered on a tablet dated 176 B.C.*

▶ *Played by the ancient Egyptians, senet was a race game similar to the royal game of Ur. Judging by the number of boards found in tombs and depicted in paintings, senet and related games such as the game of twenty were an important part of Egyptian culture.*

CULTURAL CONTACT

The discovery of similar board games around the world reveals that even thousands of years ago diverse cultures were coming into contact with each other and sharing ideas and customs. For example, the distinctive nine men's morris board (see pages 10–11) has been discovered at the farthest western end of Europe, in Ireland, as well as all over Asia.

◀▲ *Historians have suggested a link between mazes (above) and board games such as nine men's morris (left). In ancient cultures both mazes and board games were thought to have magical powers.*

MANCALA ON THE MOVE

Another game that spread far and wide is mancala (see pages 30–33). Its origins are African, but it is now played throughout most of the world. The Arabs took the game along their trading routes into Asia—versions of mancala have been found in China, Sri Lanka, and the Philippines. African slaves carried the game west to the Americas.

CHANGING CHESS

From its beginnings in central Asia chess traveled far to the east and west. The game changed little by little, to improve playing or just to suit the particular culture that played it. In the east China and Japan have their own forms of chess that are just as ancient as the Western—and now international—form of the game.

Unfortunately chess and backgammon became so popular across Europe in the Middle Ages that other games were neglected. For example hnefatafl was popular throughout the Viking world (Scandinavia, Iceland, and parts of Great Britain and Ireland) for over 700 years until around A.D. 1100.

▶ This hnefatafl board dates from the A.D. 900s. It was discovered in Ballinderry, Ireland. A king was placed in the center protected by dark-colored guards. Around the outside of the board stood light-colored attackers whose goal was to capture the king. The king's aim, with the aid of its guards, was to find a safe path to the side of the board.

FROM ALQUERQUE TO CHECKERS

Another effect of the popularity of chess was that other games were transferred on to a checkered board. Checkers, for example, derives from alquerque, a much older game than chess.

◀ The Arabs were the first people to take chess seriously. This illustration is from a 14th-century manuscript.

◀ Alquerque pieces were placed on the intersecting points of this netlike grid. When people began playing the game on a chessboard, the pieces were placed in the squares, but the diagonal movements remained.

NINE MEN'S MORRIS

Nine men's morris has been played for thousands of years by cultures all over the world, from ancient Egypt to China and from Troy to Neolithic Ireland.

The reason for the game's long-term popularity is its simple form. You can scratch the shape of a board in the ground, pick up some pebbles, and play. Nine men's morris is best described as a complicated version of ticktacktoe (tic-tac-toe). One of your aims is to form a line of three pieces. This allows you to permanently remove one of your opponent's pieces from the board.

Did you know?

The word "morris" has nothing to do with morris dancing—traditional old English display dancing. It comes from the Latin word merellus, which means a counter or a game piece. Nine men's morris was one of many board games played by the Romans.

Black's move has blocked White's attempt to form a row of three.

1

MOVING AND WINNING

There are two ways to win—either by blocking your opponent's pieces so that they cannot move or by leaving your opponent with just two pieces, making it impossible to form a line of three.

The game falls into two phases. In phase one the two players take turns placing nine pieces on the board, one by one. Pieces are placed on the points where lines intersect **(diagram 1)**.

After all of the 18 pieces have been placed on the board, phase two begins. The players maneuver their pieces, still taking turns, and try to form a line of three. Pieces are moved one step along the lines to the next point as long as it is vacant **(diagram 2)**.

Black moves a piece, ready to form a line of three on the next turn.

2

THREE IN A ROW

If you manage to make a row of three pieces along a straight line, you can remove any one of your opponent's pieces, as long as it is not part of a line of three. A piece from a line of three can only be captured if there are no other pieces available.

The line of three cannot be used to take another enemy piece on your next turn. First one of your three men must move away and then roll back into position on the next turn. Be careful that your opponent does not block the line when you move away. If you are skillful enough, you might be able to create a lethal formation—two rolling lines of three (**diagram 3**).

Black breaks one row of three and, at the same time, forms another. On Black's next turn the piece rolls back again. Each time, White loses a piece and cannot easily fight back.

3

VARIATIONS

There are many different versions of nine men's morris. Some use fewer pieces, and some use more. Board designs vary too. Try out these versions to see which one you like the best. The rules are essentially the same as for the nine man game—forming a row of three is the objective.

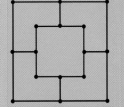
Five men's morris

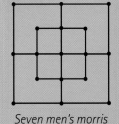
Seven men's morris

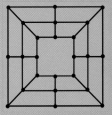
Twelve men's morris

FOX AND GEESE

Fox and Geese is a "chase game." The two opposing forces have unequal powers and different objectives. The pack of geese have to trap the fox so that it cannot move, but the fox will win the game if it remains free. Fox and Geese is a test of nerves. If the geese rush forward too quickly, they will be doomed; the lone fox has to wait patiently for the geese to show weakness.

SETTING UP

The 13 geese are arranged as shown below. The fox can start on any vacant point, but somewhere in the center is advisable. This allows the fox to cover all sides of the board. The player with the geese makes the first move, then the two sides take turns.

▼ *Fox and Geese is played on a round or cross-shaped board. The 13 geese (red) are placed at one end of the board, and the single fox (blue) is usually placed in the center.*

MOVING

Fox and Geese is easiest to play on a board with lines, which show where the pieces are allowed to move. A goose may move one space at a time in any direction (forward, backward, sideways, or diagonally) to the nearest unoccupied point but only along the lines. Geese cannot jump over each other or the fox. The fox moves in the same way along the lines, but it is able to capture geese by leaping over them if it has the chance.

1

Here the goose in the center could move directly forward, diagonally forward, or to either side. Going forward would not be a good idea—the piece could be taken. It would be better to move up one of the geese from the pack as shown.

The fox captures a goose by leaping over it along a straight line to an unoccupied point on the other side. More than one goose may be captured in a single move.

2

▶ *With this last move the geese have trapped the fox and won the game.*

STRATEGY

The geese must work together, protecting each other from being captured. Try not to let a goose be separated from the pack or else the fox could hunt it down. Edge up the board slowly, gradually restricting the fox's territory. At the start of the game several geese at the back of the pack will not be involved. Try to bring them into the game as soon as possible—only by using all of the geese can you hope to trap the fox.

If you are the fox, look for weaknesses in the opposition. Remember that you cannot be caught so if you spy an opening in the pack, slip into it. It is almost impossible to be trapped in the center of the board, so the fox can make daring raids without risk. Attack lone geese—even if you cannot force a capture, keeping the geese occupied with defending themselves will upset their plans.

BACKGAMMON

Backgammon is fast moving and treacherous. Two players race game pieces around the board—the first to guide them home and out is the winner. Although this is a game of great strategic skill the rules are relatively simple.

THE AIM

The aim of backgammon is to remove all your pieces (counters) from the board before your opponent can. To do this you have to bring the counters into the home board.

SETTING UP

Each player begins with 15 counters. One side, for example, may have white and the other black. The counters are always set up in the same way at the start of the game.

Black sits here

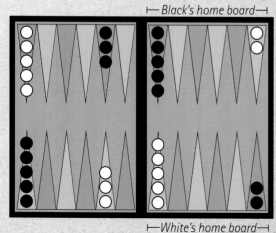

White moves in this direction

├─ *Black's home board* ─┤

The counters are placed on points. On many boards the points are alternately colored, but that has no bearing on the game. These two diagrams show how the board looks at the start of a game.

├─*White's home board*─┤

Black moves in this direction

BEGINNING THE GAME

Each player throws a die. The player with the higher score begins, using the scores from both dice. After that the players take turns moving, rolling two dice at a time.

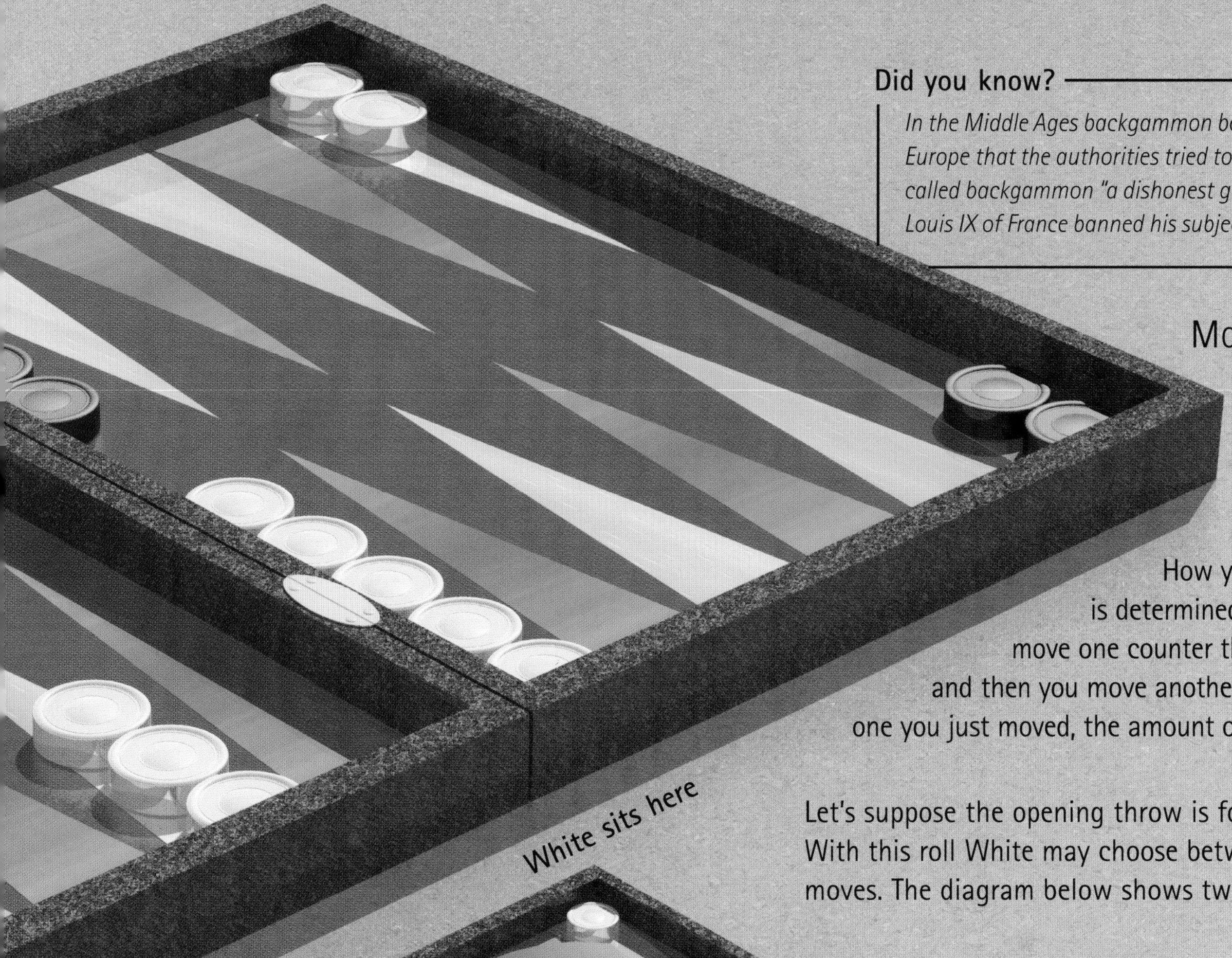

MOVING THE COUNTERS

The counters move along the points toward their home board. Counters can only move forward. How you move your counters is determined by the dice throw. You move one counter the amount on one die, and then you move another counter, or the same one you just moved, the amount on the other die.

Let's suppose the opening throw is four and two (4-2). With this roll White may choose between several different moves. The diagram below shows two of the possibilities.

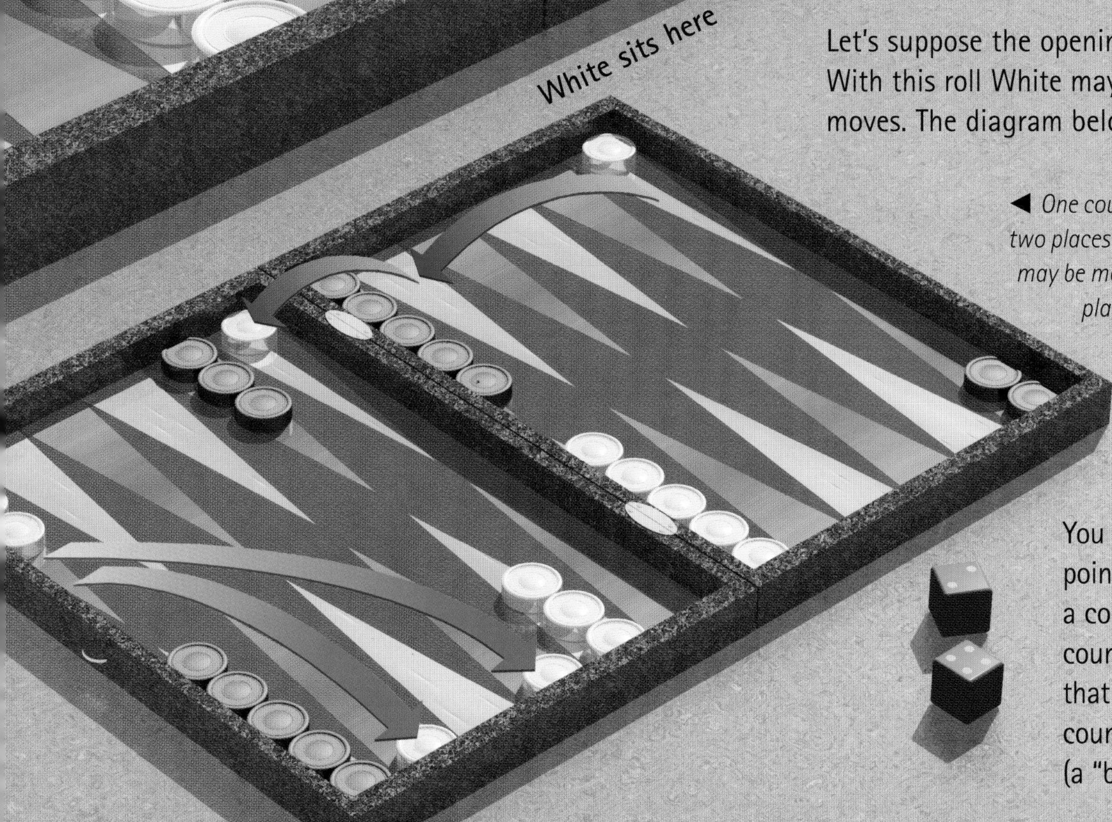

White sits here

◄ *One counter may move four places, followed by two places (the move shown in blue). Or two counters may be moved—one four places and another two places (shown in green). If you throw a double, this is treated as four times the score on one die—four 6s, for example. This throw can be used in different ways, as long as all the 6s are used.*

You may move a counter to an empty point or to one where you already have a counter. If there are two opposition counters together, you cannot occupy that point with one of your own counters. A single opposition counter (a "blot") on a point can be captured.

HITS, BLOTS, AND BEARING OFF

When a backgammon counter is "hit" (captured) it does not leave the board for good. It sits on the central bar before returning to play via the opponent's home board.

Hitting plays an important role in backgammon— it slows down your opponent since a captured counter must restart the journey back to its own home board **(diagrams 1–3)**.

— Black's home board —

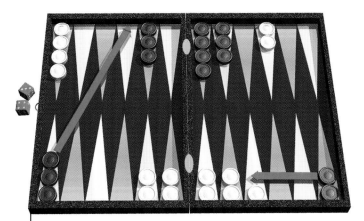

1 *In this position a dice throw of 4-3 allows Black to use the 3 to hit White's unprotected "blot" (a single counter). The two White counters next to it are safe, so Black has to use the 4 in another way, as shown.*

2 *After being hit the White counter is placed on the bar— the ridge in the center of the board. Before White can make any other move this counter must reenter the game via Black's home board.*

6 5 4 3 2 1

3 *When you return a counter to the board, think of the points as numbered from one to six. Imagine White now throws 5-2. The five-point position is already occupied by Black counters, but the two-point position is vacant—so the White counter returns on the two-point, and the 5 is used elsewhere. If White had thrown a double 5 or a double 6, the counter would not have been able to return to the board, and it would be Black's turn.*

If one side has several counters on the bar, they must all reenter the opponent's home board before any other counters are able to move.

FINISHING THE GAME

The first player to "bear off" (or remove) all of their counters from the board wins the game. Before bearing off can begin a player must move their counters into the home board **(diagrams 4 and 5)**.

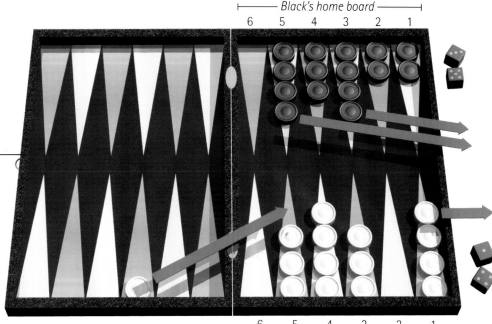

4

With all the Black counters inside of the home board, Black is ready to begin bearing off. If Black throws 5-3, two counters can be removed—one from the five-point and one from the three-point.

White is now behind in the race. Before bearing off can begin one last counter must be brought into the home board. Imagine White rolls 4-1. The last counter is brought inside of the home board with the 4, and the 1 is used to bear off a counter from the one-point. The race is on.

5

Black's next throw is a double 6—a great stroke of luck. Remember, a double gives you four times the score on one die, so Black has four 6s to use. The six-point is empty, so Black bears off from the next point down—three counters are removed from the five-point. The five-point is now empty, so the final 6 is used to bear off a counter from the four-point.

White has less luck with a roll of 6-2. As we have seen the 6 can be used to bear off a counter from the five-point, but the two-point is empty. White cannot bear off from the one-point since there are still counters above the two-point. Instead White uses the 2 to fill the space on the two-point, making sure that two counters will bear off on the next throw.

Let's review. Black has taken off six counters, and White has only removed two. Black will probably win the race, but if White were to throw a couple of doubles, the game could still turn around.

POINTS AND PRIMES

The ultimate aim in backgammon is to bear off your pieces before your opponent does. This might cause you to think that the strategy is simple—you charge your counters around the board, and the dice decide who crosses the finishing line first. In fact a straight race is very rare. The best backgammon players combine the efficient movement of their own counters with the restriction of their opponent's pieces.

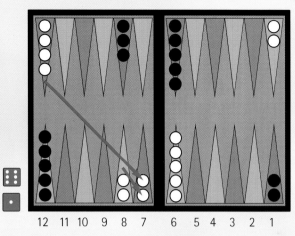

1 *With an opening roll of 6-1 White occupies the seven-point. At some point Black's two back counters (on the one-point) must make a move back to their own home board. This becomes harder when there is a barrier to jump over.*

BUILDING SECURE POINTS

We have already seen that hitting your opponent's pieces is one way to slow down their progress, but that depends on the luck of the dice. Another way is to create secure points around the board.

Imagine White's opening dice roll is 6-1. This is one of the most useful rolls at the start of the game because it allows White to "build" (occupy) the important seven-point position **(diagram 1)**. Building secure points not only limits your opponent's mobility but also provides safe stepping-stones for your own counters on the difficult journey back to the home board.

THE SIX-POINT PRIME

The six-point prime is a highly effective blocking strategy. It is formed by building six secure points in a row **(diagram 2)**.

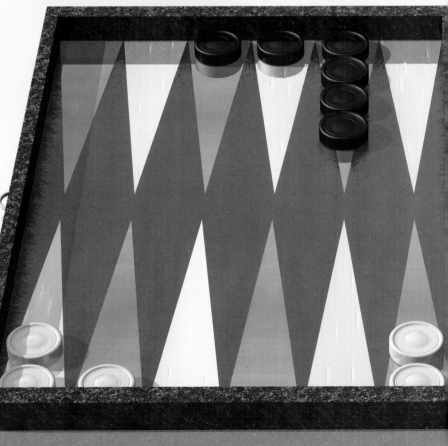

Here White has built a six-point prime. Black's two back counters are unable to jump over White's six secure points, so they are trapped. Over the next few moves White leaves the blocking "prime" in position and brings the rest of the counters into the home board. Even if the two Black counters in the corner finally do escape (after White brings the two counters on the seven-point into the home board), then White will be far ahead in the race to bear off.

THE GOLDEN POINT

How can you prevent your two back counters from becoming blockaded? Charging both pieces around the board to safety is a risky strategy. Even if one piece makes it, the other could be stranded, then hit and blocked by incoming opposing counters. An alternative tactic is to secure a foothold farther up in your opponent's home board—on the five-point, for example **(diagrams 3 and 4)**. Because of its strategic importance, the five-point is known as the "golden point."

─ Black's home board ─
6 5 4 3 2 1

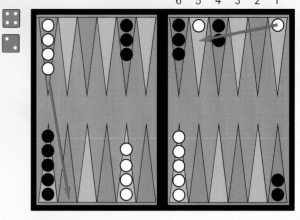

3 *Here White has already moved one of the back counters up to the five-point. White now rolls 4-2 and uses the 4 to occupy the five-point. From here it is easier for White's two back counters to make a break for safety. They are also in a good position to hit stray Black blots, and they provide a safe point for other White counters returning from the bar.*

─ Black's home board ─
6 5 4 3 2 1

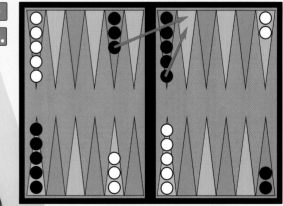

4 *If your opening roll is 3-1, occupy the "golden point" in your home board. Not only is it the first step in restricting your opponent's back counters, but it also prevents them from building on the five-point themselves.*

── Black's home board ──

── White's home board ──

Go

The game of go has an appealing simplicity. One side plays with white stones and the other with black. The opposing sides try to surround each other in a subtle struggle. In chess or checkers games can be won by a lightning attack. Patience and a calm overview of the board are the key tactics of a go player.

CHINESE ORIGINS

The game began in China, possibly as early as 2000 B.C. Ancient texts describe the board in astrological terms, suggesting that go developed from a way of predicting the future from the stars.

The Japanese took go to a new level of sophistication in the era of the Tokugawa shoguns, or warrior rulers (1603–1867). Schools were set up to develop the theory of the game, which was thought to provide excellent moral, intellectual, and strategic training.

GLOBAL GO

Go is now played all over the world, although it is most popular in China, Japan, and South Korea. In Japan there are more than 400 professional players. Go has a ranking system similar to that of karate—apprentice professionals start at 1 dan and attempt to work their way up to the highest title of 9 dan.

▼ Go is a game for two players. Tournament games are played on a board of 19 horizontal and 19 vertical lines. The black dots act as markers to help players judge where to lay their stones.

STARTING THE GAME

The board is empty at the start of the game. Black has 181 stones, and White has 180 stones—although it is very rare that all of them are used. Stones are not placed in the squares but instead on the points where lines intersect. Black always plays first, then the players take turns. Once a stone is placed it cannot be moved, but it can be captured.

THE AIM

The aim in go is to surround a larger amount of territory than your opponent. The game ends when both players feel that they cannot gain any more territory or capture any more stones. Players score one point for each empty intersection inside of their own territory, and one point for every stone they have captured. The player with the higher total is the winner.

◀ *At the end of this game on a small board White has surrounded 19 points of intersection (the white crosses), and Black has surrounded 16 points (the black crosses). White captured two stones, and Black captured three. Adding up the totals White has 21 points, and Black has 19 points. White is the winner.*

LIBERTIES, GROUPS, AND EYES

Although the chief aim in go is to surround as much territory as possible, capturing enemy stones could help you achieve that goal. Captured stones also count toward your score at the end of the game.

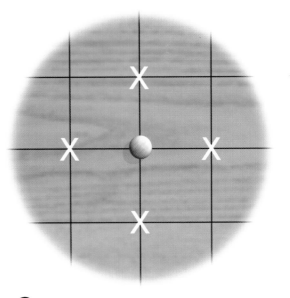

1 *The crosses show the White stone's liberties. A stone needs at least one liberty to survive.*

LIBERTIES

A stone in the middle of the board has four open points around it. These are called "liberties" **(diagram 1)**. In order to capture that stone enemy stones must occupy all four points **(diagram 2)**.

2 *Here three of the White stone's liberties have been taken (A). To capture the White stone Black places a stone on the last liberty (B). The White stone is removed from the board (C).*

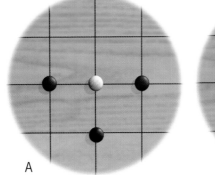

A　　　　　B　　　　　C

Stones can also be captured at the sides and in the corners of the board **(diagrams 3 and 4)**.

3 *At the side of the board a stone only has three liberties. Black captures the White stone by playing a stone, as shown.*

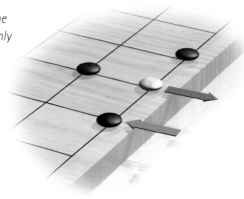

4 *In the corner a stone only has two liberties. Placing a Black stone, as shown, captures the White stone in the corner.*

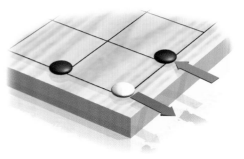

GROUPS

Forming groups of stones can be a good way to enclose territory and protect your stones. A group of stones can be captured, but to do so the entire group must be surrounded and all of its liberties closed (diagrams 5–7).

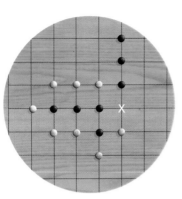

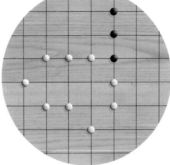

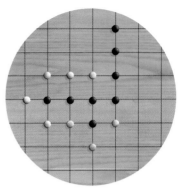

5 In this position the point marked with a cross is especially important. It is called the "cutting point."

6 If White is to play, placing a stone on the cutting point surrounds and captures the group of four Black stones.

7 A Black stone laid on the cutting point forms a strong chain. With several isolated stones White is now in the weaker position.

EYES

In order to create a completely secure group of stones that group has to enclose two vacant points, or "eyes" (diagram 8). A group with just one eye is vulnerable to capture (diagram 9).

9 A group with one eye is not secure. Here it would be legal for White to place a stone on the eye in the middle of the Black group. Again the White stone will be surrounded by Black stones, but this time the move will close off the Black group's last liberty. The Black stones will be captured.

8 Here the Black stones are safe from capture because the group contains two eyes (marked with crosses). It is illegal for White to place a stone on either of the two eyes because that stone would have no liberties.

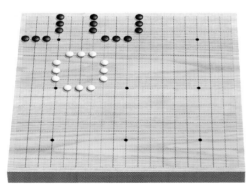

STRATEGY

In professional games the struggle often revolves around the corners. Diagram 10 illustrates why.

10 Each group of stones encloses the same amount of territory—nine points. In the middle 12 stones are needed to do this. At the side it is nine stones. In the corner only six stones are required. In other words territory can be enclosed more efficiently at the corners of the board.

(Test position)

Solution on pages 58–59

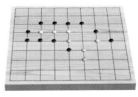

How can Black capture five White stones to play? Think a few moves ahead to find the answer.

CHESS

▲ *The Isle of Lewis chess pieces date back to the 1100s. Carved from walrus ivory, they form the oldest surviving complete set.*

Chess is a game of war in which the fate of your army depends entirely on your own skill. In other games moves are often determined by the roll of a dice or the turn of a card. But luck has no part in chess. This, combined with the game's complexity, explains why chess can be one of the most satisfying games of all to win.

CHESS ON THE MOVE

Chess first emerged in northern India before spreading to the Arab world. By the Middle Ages it had become the most popular game in Europe. Chess is now played worldwide by millions of people. The number of players continues to grow with the popularity of chess sites on the Internet.

| Rook | Knight | Bishop | King | Queen | Pawn |

▲ *In chess diagrams each piece is represented by a symbol. Don't mix up the king and queen—the king is the taller of the two pieces and has a cross on top.*

SETTING UP

Chess is played by two players on a board of 64 squares. Half of the squares are white (or a light color) and the other half are black (or a dark color). One player commands the white pieces, the other the black, and they take turns moving their pieces. White always makes the first move.

At the beginning of the game position the board so that there is a white square at the bottom right-hand corner. Then set up the pieces. On the first row of squares (or "rank") place the most important pieces. The rooks sit in the corners. Next to them on both sides of the board are the knights. Then come the bishops and finally, on the middle two squares, stand the queen and king.

Did you know?

No one knows how the game of chess began. It is not clear whether it was invented by one person or whether several different games gradually merged into one. The earliest references to chess date from around A.D. 600—making chess a relatively young game compared to backgammon and go.

Be sure to put the king and queen on the correct squares. There is an easy rule to help you—the queen stands on its own color. In other words, if you have a White queen, place it on the white square closest to the middle. If you have a Black queen, stand it on the black square closest to the middle. In front of these pieces, on the second rank, is a row of eight pawns.

◀▼ *The pieces always stand in the same position at the start of the game. Make sure that king faces king and queen faces queen.*

THE PIECES

The best way to learn how the pieces move is by practicing with them on an empty chessboard. Move the pieces one at a time, mastering each one's unique movement before starting a full game.

❶

THE KING ♔

The king is the tallest chess piece. It always has a cross on top of its crown. The whole game revolves around trying to trap the king into checkmate (see pages 28–29). That makes it the most important piece on the board, but the king is actually one of the least powerful. It only moves one square at a time in any direction.

❷

THE BISHOP ♗

A bishop may move forward or backward along the diagonals for as many squares as it likes, as long as there is nothing standing in the way. Both sides have two bishops— one moves along the dark squares of the board, the other along the light squares.

THE ROOK ♖

The rook is a powerful piece and moves in a straight line up and down and from side to side for as many squares as it likes— unless something is blocking its path. Rooks cannot leap over other pieces except when they perform the special move of "castling" (see page 27).

❸

❹ ### THE QUEEN ♕

The queen has a crown on top of the piece and is a little shorter than the king, which it stands next to at the start of battle. The queen is the most powerful piece on the board. It moves up and down and from side to side across the board like the rook, as well as along the diagonals like the bishop—as long as nothing is blocking its path.

THE PAWN ♟

On its first move a pawn can advance either two squares or one (A). After this it can only move forward one square at a time (B). Pawns capture in a different way as compared to how they normally move—by advancing one square diagonally forward. Here, for example, the pawn in front of the rook and the knight could take either piece (C). If a pawn reaches the far side of the board, it changes into a rook, knight, bishop, or queen (D). Most players choose a queen because it is the most powerful piece on the board.

THE KNIGHT ♞

The knight moves in an "L" shape—two squares in a straight line and then one to the left or right. The knight makes the game more dynamic. In positions that seem blocked it can force a breakthrough because it is the only piece that can leap over other pieces. Here, for example, the knight in the corner can capture the bishop on the other side of the pawns.

5

SPECIAL MOVES—CASTLING

Castling is a good way to protect your king and also move a powerful piece, the rook, into battle. In short castling the king moves two squares toward the closest rook. The rook leaps over the king, landing next to it. In long castling the king moves two squares toward the farthest rook. The rook jumps over the king and lands next to it. There are a few rules to remember—you cannot castle if your king or rook has already moved, if your king is in check, if your king will land into a check, or if a piece is standing between the king and rook.

Short castling

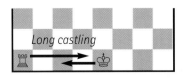

Long castling

SPECIAL MOVES—EN PASSANT

This special method of pawn capture is only available in a particular situation. When a pawn advances two squares from its starting position, an enemy pawn standing next to it on the fifth rank can capture it. In this example the White pawn moves one square diagonally behind the Black pawn and removes it from the board. It is as if the Black pawn had only moved one square. An "en passant" capture must be made during the turn immediately after the enemy pawn has moved two squares, otherwise the option disappears.

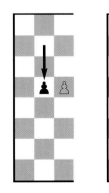

Did you know?

Many players like to announce "check," but in the rules of the game it is not necessary to do so. Often a player says it just to upset the opponent!

White's king is under attack from the rook. We say that the king is in check. The king must move out of check immediately. The only option is to move forward one square.

1

Board Games—Chess

CHECK AND CHECKMATE

The ultimate aim in a game of chess is to checkmate your opponent's king. The term comes from the ancient Persian *shah mat*, which means "the king is defeated."

To achieve checkmate, you must threaten the enemy king with one of your pieces so that the king is unable to move and escape capture. Normally a checkmate occurs when one side has an overwhelming superiority in forces or through a direct and unexpected assault on the king.

Checking occurs when the king is attacked but can still escape. In other words, it is not fatal. Diagrams 1 and 2 demonstrate what the terms mean.

WHY CHECK?

Don't panic if you suddenly find yourself in check. The game is not over, and it does not always benefit your opponent. So what is the point of checking?

- A check can help you gain time.

- Checking can drive the enemy king to a poor square, leaving it open to further attack.

TEST POSITIONS

In order to make sure you understand the concepts of check and checkmate here are two test positions to solve. Work out whether it is check or checkmate, and if it is only check, how do you escape? The solutions are on pages 58–59.

2

White's king is in check again from the rook, but this time there is no escape. The king is trapped by its own pawns and cannot move out of check so we say it is checkmated. The game is over, and Black has won!

(solutions are on pages 58–59)

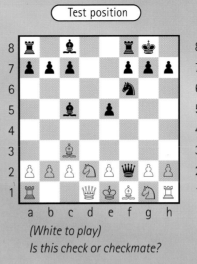

Test position

(White to play)
Is this check or checkmate?

Test position

(Black to play)
Is this check or checkmate?

Did you know?

If you fail to see that you are in check and do not prevent the attack to your king, it does not mean that you lose the game. Your opponent has to let you make your move again to get out of check.

STALEMATE

This is when a player cannot make any legal moves but is not in check. It usually occurs when one side has an overwhelming advantage and is moving in for a checkmate against an exposed king (**diagram 3**).

3

With a king and queen against a lone king, White aims for a quick checkmate. The queen closes in for the kill but comes slightly too close. Black's king has no legal moves but is not checkmated. This position is stalemate, and the game is a tie.

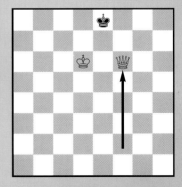

MANCALA

Mancala is the most popular board game in Africa. It is a game of pure skill. To do well you have to think fast and be able to plan ahead for many moves.

In African communities mancala is a social game. Spectators often join in, suggesting or even making moves. Mancala is very complicated, so you can spend a long time thinking over each position, trying to calculate all the different possibilities. But in Africa the game is traditionally fast and furious.

▲ *Although a mancala board can be made very easily, many boards are expertly carved. This board in the shape of a wheelbarrow is from Sierra Leone, in Africa.*

BOARDS AND BEANS

Mancala boards are usually carved from wood, but a simple board can be made by scooping holes out of sand or earth. The playing pieces are made of almost anything, as long as they are roughly the same size and pleasant to hold—nuts, beans, pebbles, or shells, for example. In other words, with a little resourcefulness, you can play mancala anywhere.

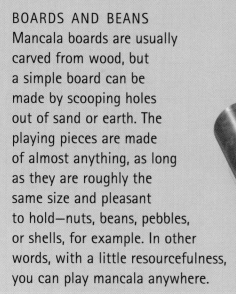

Large hole to store beans captured by player two

Player two sits here

Player one sits here

SETTING UP

The two players sit on each side of the board. Each of the 12 holes is filled with four beans, making 48 beans in all. A larger cup at each end is used to store captured beans. Players take turns moving.

THE AIM

The aim in mancala is to win the most beans, so when one player has won more than half of the beans (more than 25), the game finishes. If both players win 24 beans, the game is a tie.

Did you know?

Some people believe that mancala developed from an early abacus. Others think it was used to predict the future. With its theme of seed sowing, mancala may even have been the invention of a farmer with a fertile mind!

Large hole to store beans captured by player one

MOVING

To begin the game a player scoops up all of the beans from any hole on their side of the board. Starting with the next hole on the right, the beans are dropped one at a time into each hole in a counterclockwise direction, using the opponent's side of the board as well. When all four beans have been distributed, the turn finishes. Players take turns to sow beans in this way.

▲ *Here player one has started the game by scooping four beans from the second hole on the right.*

▶ *From ancient to modern— some cell phones now feature a version of mancala.*

CAPTURING BEANS

To make a capture in mancala you need to finish sowing on your opponent's side of the board in a hole that contains one or two beans only (making the total two or three beans after sowing).

Player two

Player one

Here player two has two holes that contain one or two beans. These holes are vulnerable. Player one can use this weakness by sowing nine beans from the hole on the far left.

1

The last sowing hole now holds two beans. These are captured and placed in player one's store. The hole just before now contains three beans so these are also captured. But the next hole back now contains four beans—these are safe from capture and player one's turn ends.

2

MANCALA RULES

If you sow from a hole containing 12 or more beans, you will make a full circuit of the board. When you reach the hole where you started, skip over it and continue sowing at the next hole.

If there are no beans left on your opponent's side of the board, if possible you should sow beans on to that side so that your opponent can make a move on their next turn.

If there are just a few beans left on the board and it is clear that no further captures can be made, the game is stopped. The remaining beans are not counted, and the player with the largest number of beans in their store is the winner.

Player two

Player one

Although player two has no holes containing one or two beans, player one can create targets with a huge lap of the board. Fifteen beans are scooped from the hole on the far right. Remember, a bean cannot be sown into the hole from which it was originally scooped.

3

4

Player one's circuit of the board has created pots of two in the previously empty holes. Player one captures the beans from four holes.

STRATEGY

As we have seen, leaving one or two beans in a hole on your side of the board can be dangerous. If that happens, continue sowing the beans or sow into the hole to create a greater number. A good strategy is to build up a large number of beans in one of your holes. If you time it right, sowing the beans around the board can be an effective method of attack (diagrams 3 and 4).

(Test positions)

Solutions on pages 58–59

What move should player two make?

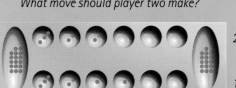

What move should player one make?

CHECKERS

Checkers is one of the most underrated games in the world. Because it is played on the same checkered board, it is often assumed to be an inferior version of chess. But the games are very different, and checkers is far more complex than its simple rules suggest.

THE AIM

One way to win a game of checkers is to capture all of your opponent's pieces (counters). Another way is to immobilize them—in other words, if you make a move but your opponent cannot, you win the game.

▲ Sometimes it is possible to capture several counters in one turn. Here the Black piece can leap over and capture two opposition pieces.

▶ Each side has 12 counters, which are placed on the dark squares. Black always begins and players take turns moving.

MOVING AND CAPTURING

The pieces may move one square diagonally forward to the left or right—but they cannot move backward. Counters capture opposing pieces by leaping over them diagonally and occupying the space on the other side. When a counter is captured, it is removed from the board. If you can take ("jump") a counter, then you have to do so.

Did you know?

Checkers has been played in Europe since the end of the 1100s, but it is probably descended from a far older game, "Alquerque," which dates back thousands of years to ancient Egypt.

KINGS

When a counter reaches the end of the board, it automatically becomes a king, and the player's move finishes. The piece is crowned by placing a counter of the same color on top of it (diagram 2). Kings move and capture in the same way as ordinary counters, but they do so by going both forward and backward. This makes them far more powerful than ordinary pieces.

▲ *Black has just played a piece to the end of the board, and it now becomes a king. On Black's next turn the king threatens to leap backward, capturing the White piece.*

2

TRICKS AND TRAPS

White spots a serious weakness in Black's forces and finds a way to exploit it. White plays a piece forward. According to the rules of the game, Black has to capture.

1

With its simple moves, you might think that checkers is a slow and straightforward game. In fact, danger lurks at every turn. One false move can lead to instant disaster, your forces crushed with no hope of recovery.

The "must capture" rule gives checkers its intrigue and complexity. It is the basis for some deadly traps such as this example from early on in a game (**diagrams 1–3**).

2

Black's forced move sets up a spectacular series of leaps. White jumps over three of Black's pieces in one turn. The move finishes at the end of the board, where White's piece becomes a king.

3

White gave up one piece but captured three in return and gained a king. Such an advantage should be more than enough for White to win the game.

WATCH THE GAP!

To avoid this type of trap, some players keep the back checkers on their starting positions for as long as possible. This is a fair strategy, but it can be limiting—eventually the back checkers must move forward to support the front pieces. Keeping a tight position is often a better tactic. As we have seen, leaving gaps between pieces can lead to disaster.

LETHAL ATTACKS

As well as watching out for the "must take" rule shown in diagrams 1–3, keep an eye out for other kinds of tactics. Here are three of the most common attacks in checkers (diagrams 4–6).

4 THE FORK
The Black king has just moved behind the two White pieces, attacking both. White can save one piece but not both.

5 INFILTRATION
This is similar to the fork in that two pieces are attacked at the same time. In this case the attacker forces its way in between the enemy pieces. White cannot avoid losing one piece.

DOMINATION
Be careful when playing your pieces on the side of the board, especially at the end of a game. They will have more limited movement than on an open board and could be dominated and trapped. In this example the Black king's move helps trap both of White's kings at the same time. The best White can do is give up one king to free the other. This leaves Black with two kings against one and a fairly simple win.

6

TEST POSITIONS

There are many subtle and beautiful finishes in checkers. Test your skill with the two problem positions below. The solutions are on pages 58–59.

The solutions are on pages 58–59.

Test position

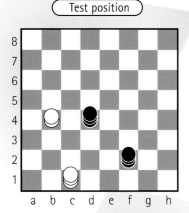

(White is playing down the board. Black to play and win)

Black has a clever way of forcing White to self-destruct in this position. You need to think ahead for several moves in order to solve this problem.

Test position

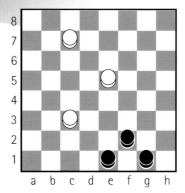

(White is playing down the board. Black to play and win)

With a piece close to becoming a king, White seems to have a good chance of winning. But Black finds an unexpected way to turn the game around. Think ahead for several moves to find the solution.

▲ *These playing cards from the Ottoman Empire are the direct ancestors of our modern packs of cards. Like ours, Ottoman packs also contained 52 cards and four suits. They came to Europe along trade routes through Spain and Italy.*

▲ *No one knows when and where playing cards first appeared, but Chinese money cards existed before European cards. The four Chinese suits were coins, strings, myriads, and tens. The designs on the cards were copied from paper money of the Tang Dynasty (A.D. 618–907).*

INTRODUCTION

Playing cards first arrived in Europe in the 1370s from the Middle East. Card games spread quickly throughout the continent. By the 1400s the craze for cards had been established among all levels of society.

WORD OF MOUTH

Card games are true "folk" games. In other words, they are generally spread by word of mouth—between family generations, for example. This accounts for the large variation in rules for many card games. Even when the "standard version" of a game is written down, it rarely maintains this form for very long. That applies to this book, too. If you think you can improve the rules for the games given here, then do so.

◄ *A European king and his courtiers enjoy a game of cards in this illustration from a medieval manuscript.*

Tip

All of the card games described in this book are played with a standard 52-card pack.

FRENCH SUITS AND FACE CARDS

The 52-card pack that is standard in the English-speaking world—and increasingly throughout the world—derives from France. It features the French suits of clubs, diamonds, hearts, and spades. The designs date back to medieval times and have barely changed in 500 years.

The king, queen, and jack are known as "face cards" or "picture cards." To today's players the designs look a little rough. They were originally printed from woodcuts, and the same pictures have remained to the present day. The origin of the king and queen is obvious, but the jack is less straightforward. This card was originally known as the "knave" (a male servant). When letters were added to the cards to help with identification, it was too confusing to have "K" for king and "Kn" for knave. Another name for the card took over— "Jack," one of the most common names at that time.

▼ *The jack, queen, and king are known as face cards. In most games face cards have a high rank.*

▼ *Until the 1800s playing cards did not have numbers or letters to identify them. These French cards date from 1752. The flat look of the characters is very similar to modern-day face cards.*

▲ *The suit of diamonds in order of rank. The ace is usually ranked the highest, with the 2 (also known as the deuce) as the lowest. The word "ace" derives from the Latin word as—a coin.*

THE PACK

The standard pack has 52 cards in four different suits. There are two red suits—hearts and diamonds—and two black suits—clubs and spades. The 13 cards in each suit are usually ranked from 2 (lowest) to ace (highest). But be careful—in some games the ace ranks as the lowest card.

In most card games certain routines are followed to show that play is fair. While most people wouldn't dream of cheating, it is still important to follow these procedures. They make everyone feel comfortable, and give the game some ceremony.

SHUFFLING AND CUTTING

Before dealing a new round of cards it is customary to shuffle and cut the cards. Shuffling ensures that players do not receive similar cards and that the cards have not been put in a particular order beforehand. The player sitting to the right of the dealer then cuts the pack in two by lifting about half the cards off the pack and placing them on the table. The dealer then places the lower half of the pack on top of the others. When shuffling, the bottom card of the pack is often visible. Cutting ensures that the bottom card remains unknown.

DEALING

Cards are usually dealt facedown, one at a time, in a clockwise direction, beginning with the player to the dealer's left. No cards should be picked up from the table until all of the cards have been dealt. This makes it easier for the dealer to see how many cards have been given to each player.

▲ *Many countries have unique packs of cards— often with less than 52 cards and with different suits. These cards are from Venice, Italy, from 1758 and feature cups, swords, coins, and cudgels (clubs).*

HOLDING THE CARDS

When the correct number of cards has been dealt, players can pick them up. First arrange your cards so that you can see what you are holding at a glance. For games like whist, hearts, and spades it is best to divide the cards into their suits. Within the suits place cards in order of rank. Alternate red and black suits to avoid confusion.

Always make sure that none of the other players can see your hand. Hold your cards up, keeping them in a tight fan shape. Once you have arranged the cards in order close them in a pack in your hand, and then fan them out again by spreading the back cards underneath the top one.

▲ This 13-card hand has been arranged into alternating suits, with cards placed in order of rank.

LEARNING THE RULES

At first the rules of card games can seem confusing. Don't worry! The best way to learn the games described in this book is to have a pack of cards and play a practice game as you read—either on your own or with a friend. Soon you will gain the confidence to begin playing for real.

▼ French card makers at work in 1680. At the time many governments imposed a tax on every pack of cards that was made.

▲ Card games can be learned from an early age. As well as being a lot of fun, they are a great way to test your memory and use your math skills.

Did you know?

Many expressions from card games have entered everyday language. If someone is described as "playing their cards close to their chest," it means they keep their plans quiet.

◀ Ganjifa is the national card game of India. The cards are usually round. These cards, dating back around 200 years, are made of ivory.

FIRST CARD GAMES

Player three

Playing these simple and entertaining games will help strengthen your knowledge of the card rankings. They are also useful stepping-stones to learn for the games that follow.

Player two

▼ Here player one is about to put down a 5. The first player to shout "snap!" will win all three piles of cards facing up.

SNAP

This game is for two or more players, and the aim is to win all the cards. The cards are divided equally between the players. Players do not look at their cards but instead place them in a face-down pile called a deck. The player to left of the dealer turns over one card and starts a face-up pile beside their deck. The next player to the left does the same, and so on, around the table. If two of the cards match, such as two jacks or two 3s, the first player to shout "snap!" wins all the face-up cards. The game then continues with the player to the left of the last person to turn over a card.

If a player uses up all of their cards, they form a new deck with their face-up cards. A player who loses all their cards is out of the game. If snap is called incorrectly, that player must give a card to each of the other players.

"Speed" snap is played the same way, but the players turn over their cards at the same time.

Player one

► *"Easy" snap is a game for two players. The pack is divided, and the cards are then placed one by one on to a central pile. If the top two cards match, shout "snap!" or slap your hand down on the pile. The game works best if several sets are removed from the pack (for example, all 2s, 3s, 4s, 5s, 6s, and 7s). This increases the chance of matching cards.*

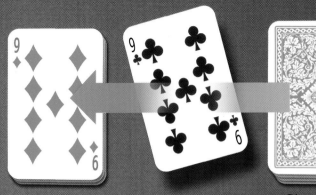

Player two

Player one

CUCKOO

This game is for three or more players, and the aim is to avoid being left with the lowest card. The cards rank from ace (lowest) to king (highest). Each player has three lives at the start of the game.

Each player is dealt one card. Players look at their own card without letting it be seen by the others. The player to the left of the dealer decides whether to keep the card or exchange it. If the card is high, he or she should keep it. Otherwise, they should put the card facedown on the table and give it to the player on their left, saying "change."

The next player can refuse to exchange if the card is a king, in which case the first player must keep their own card. But if not, he or she must exchange. Now player two decides whether to keep or exchange cards with the person on their left, and so on. When it is the dealer's turn, if he or she wishes to exchange, they cut the pack and take the top card from the lower half. If the card is a king, he or she loses the round and a life.

► *After the exchanges the players show their cards. The player with the lowest card loses a life. Here players five and six tie for the lowest card, so they both lose a life. Because player five has lost their third life, they drop out. The last player left in the game is the winner.*

Player five

Player four

Player six

Player three

Player two

Player one

RUMMY

Rummy became popular in the U.S. around 100 years ago and was played by many people working in the Hollywood movie industry. It was the perfect game to play during breaks in filming since hands can move fast.

THE AIM

The aim in rummy is to get rid of all of your cards by melding. A "meld" is a set of three or more cards—either three or four of a kind or a run of three or more cards of the same suit in order of rank **(diagram 1)**. Aces are low, so the lowest possible run is A-2-3. The highest is J-Q-K.

Player two

Melds

Stock pile

Player one

1 *Two examples of a meld in rummy—three of a kind (left), and a run of three hearts (right).*

THE DEAL

For a two-player game of rummy deal ten cards each. For three to five players deal seven cards each. For six players deal six cards each. The remaining cards are placed facedown to make the stock pile. The top card is turned over and placed next to the stock pile to form the discard pile.

CARD PLAY

The player on the left of the dealer begins. He or she takes either the top card from the stock pile or the upturned card from the discard pile. If he or she has any melds, they may lay them down. On later turns he or she may lay off single cards on to any existing melds on the table. A player can make as many melds and lay offs in one turn as they want. Finally the player adds a card to the discard pile. (Note—if you take a card from the discard pile, you cannot put the same card back.) The turn moves to the player to the left.

If the stock pile runs out, turn over the discards to form a new stock. Turn the top card over to make a new discard pile. The players can decide whether to shuffle the stock pile or not. Leave the cards if you want to test your memory, or shuffle them if you would like the game to be more random.

WINNING AND SCORING

The player who gets rid of their last card—either by creating a new meld, by laying off, or by a discard—wins the round **(diagram 2)**. The winner's score is the total value of the cards held by the other players. Aces count as one, face cards all score ten, and the others count as their face value **(diagram 3)**. If a player lays down their entire hand in one turn, they score double for a "rummy." After scoring, the deal passes on to the next player for a new round. Playing continues until an agreed points total, such as 200, has been reached.

Player two (24 points)

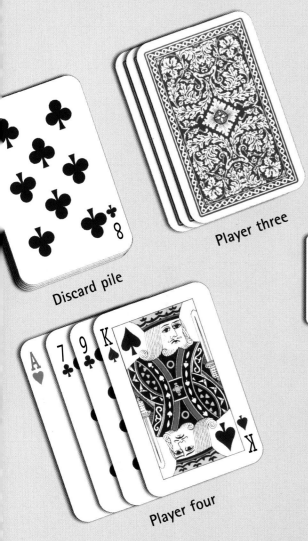

Player three

Discard pile

Player four

Player one (45 points)

Player three (25 points)

3 *After player four discards his or her last card the other players reveal their hands. Player one has 45 points, player two has 24 points, and player three has 25 points. So, player four's total score for the round is 94 points.*

Melds

2 *Here player four seizes his or her chance by taking the 8 of clubs from the discard pile. Four forms a meld with the 7, 8, and 9 of clubs, lays off the ace of hearts on the meld of three aces, and, finally, discards the king of spades. Four has no cards left, so the round is over.*

Tips

- *If you have a meld, you do not have to lay it down immediately—that might allow your opponents to lay off cards. Don't hang on to melds for too long though—you might be caught with the cards if someone else goes out.*
- *In general, discard higher scoring cards and keep lower ones. Even if you don't win the round, at least you won't give too many points to your opponents.*

CRIBBAGE

The English game of cribbage dates back to the 1600s. Once the rules are mastered it is simple—but to play well you need to be sharp to spot chances to score. Points are won with card play, and the scores are marked with pegs on a special cribbage board. You can keep score with a pen and paper if you don't have a board.

Cribbage is a two-player game in which the aim is to reach 121 points. The cards have the usual ranking, but the ace is low. Each card has a numerical value—all face cards score ten, and the rest have their face value, including the ace, which scores one. These values are important when playing the cards and scoring. Diagram 1 shows how to set up at the start of a game.

▲ Cribbage was supposedly invented by Sir John Suckling— a 17th-century adventurer, poet, and gambler—although it has its beginnings in earlier English games.

Nondealer

Turn up card

1 To start both players cut a card—the lowest card deals. Six cards are dealt to each player facedown. Each player looks at their cards and chooses two to discard. The four discards form the "crib." They remain facedown to the right of the dealer. Only the dealer uses them. Then the pack is cut again, and the top card is turned faceup on top of the pack. This is the turn up card. It is only used after the card play.

Dealer

Crib

Points are scored for card combinations in play with your opponent and at the end of card play when hands are shown. The table on page 47 shows the various scoring combinations.

COMBINATION	EXAMPLE	SCORE
Fifteen (any group of cards totaling 15)		2 points
Pair (two cards of the same rank)		2 points
Pair royal (three cards of the same rank)		6 points
Double pair royal (four cards of the same rank)		12 points
Run (a sequence of at least three cards in rank order, cards do not have to be the same suit)		1 point per card
Flush (any four or five cards of the same suit)		1 point per card

CARD PLAY

The nondealer always begins. He or she lays one of their four cards faceup on the table and announces its value. For example, if he or she lays a king they would say "ten." The dealer then plays a card, keeping it separate from the opponent's card. If the dealer has a 5, he or she should lay it down, announcing "fifteen for two points"— the total value of the cards laid so far and the number of points received. Look out for any card combinations that score points. The players take turns laying cards, each time announcing the running total and any scoring combinations.

If, by laying a card, one of the players gets a total of 31 points exactly, then they score two points. If a player would exceed 31 points by laying their next card, they stop playing and say "go." The opponent then continues laying cards until they either hit 31 (scoring two points) or cannot play without bringing the total over 31. At that point he or she announces "go" and scores a point for playing the last card.

Whenever a player hits 31, or both players have announced "go," the face-up cards are turned over, and the game restarts with the remaining cards in each player's hand. The player who did not score at the end of the play leads. The count starts again at zero, again with 31 as the target. Players must keep their own cards on one side, even though they have already been played. They will be needed in the next part of the game.

SCORING AT THE SHOW

After the card play has finished the players take their own cards back for the "show."

Each player turns his hand faceup and announces all the scoring combinations. The nondealer goes first. Both players use the "turn up card" to form combinations. After the dealer has announced the points scored from their hand, they do the same with the cards in the crib. When making combinations from the crib, there is one scoring exception—a flush can only be scored with five cards.

Diagrams 1 and 2 illustrate the scoring at the show, using the same cards dealt out on page 46.

1 *The nondealer has three scoring combinations—a pair and two runs. The total score for the hand is eight points.*

Pair (2 points)

Three-card run (3 points)   Three-card run (3 points)

Dealer's hand

Pair (2 points)

Crib

   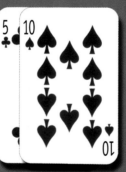      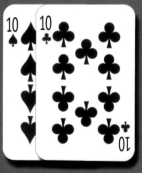

Fifteen (2 points)   Fifteen (2 points)   Fifteen (2 points)   Pair (2 points)

2 *The dealer's hand has one scoring combination—a pair. The crib gives him or her three fifteens and a pair. The dealer's total score for the round is ten points—the combined scores of the dealer's hand and the crib.*

BONUS POINTS

If the turn up card is a jack, the dealer scores two bonus points. This has to be scored before any cards are played. If either player has a jack of the same suit as the turn up card, then they score one bonus point. This should not be announced until the show.

STRATEGY

The skill in cribbage is being able to maximize your scoring opportunities while minimizing your opponent's. Following the tips below might not work out every time, but it should improve the odds.

If you are the dealer, put strong cards into the crib, but at the same time keep cards in your hand that offer good chances for you to score. It's not easy to do both, so if in doubt, favor the crib with the best cards, such as:

- two 5s
- 4 and an ace
- 5 and a card worth ten
- 5 and 6
- 6 and 9
- 2 and 3
- 7 and 8
- any pair

In the crib these cards offer scoring opportunities such as fifteen for two points or a pair for two points.

▼ A cribbage board keeps track of the game's stop-and-go. Each player has two pegs. Here Black has already scored six points, as shown by the position of the front peg in the sixth hole. If Black now scores eight points from card play, he or her counts eight holes ahead of the front peg and places the back peg there. The back peg is always used for counting, while the front peg marks the total score so far. Pegs are played first up the outer rows of holes and then down the inner rows. The player who reaches the game hole after two circuits of the board (scoring 121 points) is the winner.

Black's front peg

Black's back peg

Game hole

If you are the nondealer, lay cards into the crib that do not help with scoring. It would be a mistake to put a 5 into the crib because it could be combined with a card worth ten to make fifteen. Do not discard cards that are close together in rank such as a 7 and a 9—if the dealer puts an 8 into the crib, a run is made. So the best cards for the nondealer to lay in the crib are cards far apart such as a 2 and a 9 or a king and a 3.

When playing the first card, avoid laying a 5—there is a high chance that your opponent could have a card worth ten, making the total score fifteen and gaining two points.

WHIST

Whist is a great game on its own, but it also forms the basis of many other popular card games. If you can play whist, you have made the first step toward games such as hearts and spades (pages 52–55), and the complexity of bridge.

THE DEAL

Whist is a game for four players—two playing against two as partners. The usual rankings apply, with aces counting high. Thirteen cards are dealt out facedown to each player (diagram 1). The last card is turned up to show trumps for that hand (for example, if the last card is the 10 of diamonds, then diamonds would be trumps). The dealer leaves this card on the table until the first trick has been played. The object of the game for both partnerships is to win the most tricks.

1 *In a game of whist partners sit across from each other. Players are named after the points on a compass, with North and South playing against East and West.*

North

East

West

South

TRICKS

A "trick" is a round of cards made up of one card per player. To win a trick you have to play the highest card in that round. Each player has 13 cards, so there are 13 tricks in each hand. Diagram 2 shows how the first trick could be played.

2

The player on the left of the dealer starts by playing any one of his or her cards. Let's imagine West plays the 2 of spades. If possible the other players must "follow suit"—that means they also must play a spade. North responds with the 5 of spades. East plays the king, but South beats that with the ace. The ace is the highest card of the round, so South wins the trick. South gathers the four cards and places them at his or her side.

3 *Continuing the game, the winner of the last trick, South, must lead. South plays the queen of spades but is unlucky. As West has no spades left, he or she cannot follow suit and is allowed to lay any other card. West plays a trump card—the 3 of diamonds. The other players have to follow suit—the 7 of spades (North) and the 3 of spades (East). West wins the trick with the 3 of diamonds.*

TRUMPS

One thing changes the usual ranking order—trumps. In the hand shown in diagram 1, let's imagine that diamonds are trumps. Every single diamond then ranks higher than a card from any other suit. Diagram 3 illustrates how trump cards make the game more unpredictable.

SCORING

There are several ways of scoring, but one way, often called the "American version," is the simplest. In a hand the first six tricks won by a partnership do not score. After this each trick scores one point. So a partnership winning eight tricks would score two points. The first side to score seven points wins a game, and the first side to win two games wins the match. Partners who revoke (do not follow suit when they are able to do so) must give the opposition two points.

SPADES

Spades is very popular in North America. It is a true "folk"
game—meaning there is no single version—so make sure that
all four players are clear about the rules before starting a game.

THE DEAL
The setup is almost the same as in whist, with four players in two
partnerships. Partners sit across from each other, and 13 cards are
dealt to each player. Aces rank high, and spades are always trumps.

BIDDING
First the members of the nondealer partnership discuss how
many tricks they think they can win together. They must not
reveal anything about their hands, except for the number
of tricks each player thinks he or she might win. When
the partnership has agreed on a total number of
tricks, it is written down—this is their contract.
Then the dealer's team does the same.

A player who thinks he or she can lose every
trick may declare "nil." Their partner then
says how many tricks he or she can win
(two nil bids are not allowed). The contract
is lost if the nil bidder wins any tricks.

A "blind nil" bid is very risky.
Again you must try not to win
any tricks, but the bid has to be
made before looking at your
cards. After examining them
you may exchange two cards
with your partner. This bid
can only be made if your team
is at least 100 points behind.

◀ A typical
nil bid hand.
High cards,
such as the king
of diamonds and
the 10 and jack of
hearts, are covered
by low cards of the
same suit—so there
is a good chance of
not winning any tricks.

CARD PLAY

Card play is almost the same as in whist (see pages 50–51), except that spades are always trumps. Spades cannot be "led" (played as the first card in a trick) until a spade has been played as a trump, or one player only has spades left.

SCORING

If a team wins the number of tricks they bid, they score ten times the bid, plus one point for each "overtrick." For example, if eight tricks were bid but nine were won, the score would be (8 x 10) + 1 = 81. Picking up overtricks is known as "sandbagging" or "bagging." There is a penalty for consistent sandbagging. If a side's number of overtricks reaches ten or more, 100 points is subtracted from their score. The total number of overtricks is easy to keep track of—it is the last digit of the score. So a team with 368 points has collected eight overtricks. If, on the next hand, they were to bid five tricks but win nine, the four overtricks would bring them above ten. Their score would be 368 + 54 = 422. Subtracting 100 points brings the score back to 322. The two extra "sandbags" are carried over to the next cycle of ten. After the twentieth overtrick another 100 points would be subtracted.

For a failed contract a side loses ten points per trick bid. So if seven tricks are bid but only five are won, 70 points are subtracted from the partnership's total score.

A successful nil bid scores 100 points, plus or minus what is won or lost from the partner's bid. If four tricks are bid and won, the score would be 140 points. If a nil bid fails, 100 points are deducted from the score—but any tricks taken by the nil bidder count toward the partner's contract. Blind nil is the same but doubled to 200 points.

The first team to reach an agreed points total—usually 250 or 500—is the winner.

Test hand

Should you make a nil bid with this hand?

Test hand

How many tricks should you aim to win with this hand?

HEARTS

Hearts belongs to the same family of card games as whist and spades. It requires skill, but luck can change quickly and unexpectedly. There is plenty of room for cunning strategy, so be alert. Different versions of the game are found all over the world—"Black Maria" is the popular name in Great Britain.

1 *Each heart is worth one penalty point regardless of its face value. The queen of spades scores 13 penalty points.*

THE AIM

Card play and trick-taking are very similar to whist, but the aim of hearts is different. You must avoid winning tricks that contain hearts or the queen of spades because these incur penalty points **(diagram 1)**. Alternatively you can try to "shoot the moon"—that means winning all 14 penalty cards. Hands are played until one player reaches an agreed number of points such as 100. The winner is the player with the lowest score at that moment.

THE DEAL AND EXCHANGE

Four players are dealt 13 cards each. Aces rank high. Before play begins each player selects any three cards from their hand and passes them facedown to the player on their left. On the next deal cards are passed to the right; on the deal after that cards are exchanged between the players facing each other; and on the fourth deal no cards are exchanged. The pattern then repeats itself.

CARD PLAY

Whoever holds the 2 of clubs plays it as the first card. Just like in whist, players must follow suit if possible. There are no trumps. Penalty cards cannot be played on the first trick unless there is no other choice. Hearts can only be led once a heart has been thrown on another suit as a penalty point.

PENALTY POINTS

At the end of each hand players add up the penalty points in the tricks they have won. If a player shoots the moon by winning all 14 penalty cards, they can either subtract 26 points from their score or add 26 points to each of the opponents' scores. This is where the deviousness of the game comes in. It might seem like one player is doing badly, having picked up several penalty points. If he or she has a strong hand, however, he or she might aim to pick up all the penalty cards, leaving the opponents with a huge score.

STRATEGY

Selecting the right cards to exchange is crucial **(diagram 2)**. If you are dealt the queen of spades, should you pass it on or keep it, hoping to give someone an unpleasant surprise later on?

- If you have the queen of spades plus just one other spade, it is best to exchange the queen—if you keep it, it could easily be forced out, and you might have to take the trick and the penalty points.

- If you have the queen of spades plus at least three other spades, it is usually safe to keep the queen. The other spades can be played when spades are led, and in the meantime you should have a chance to dump the queen on an opponent once a "void" (a lack of any cards in one suit) appears in your hand.

- Unless you want to shoot the moon, keep your 2s and 3s. Leading these usually ensures that someone else wins the trick. High cards can be useful, too. The ace of hearts, for example, may stop an opponent from shooting the moon.

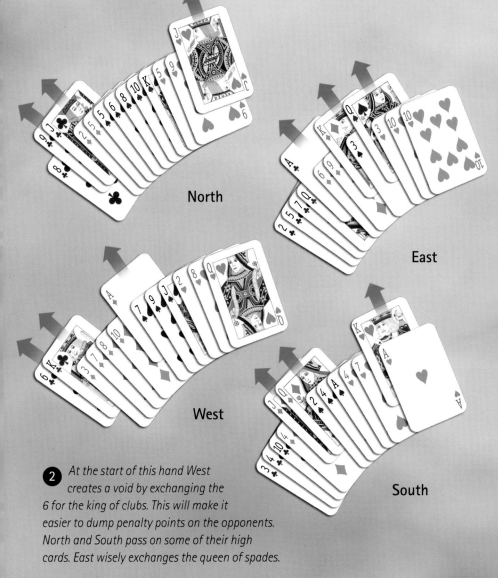

North

East

West

South

2 At the start of this hand West creates a void by exchanging the 6 for the king of clubs. This will make it easier to dump penalty points on the opponents. North and South pass on some of their high cards. East wisely exchanges the queen of spades.

BLACKJACK

This betting game is known by several names, including pontoon, twenty-one, and vingt-et-un. Each version has slightly different rules. Blackjack is the name of the version played in casinos. The game described here is very close to that and can be played at home— or anywhere!

Blackjack works best with three or more players. Cards are worth their face value, with aces worth either one or 11. The face cards are all worth ten. The suits are irrelevant. Each player starts with a fixed number of chips, or counters—let's say 30—for betting.

THE AIM

Players try to beat the dealer by ending up with cards with a total value greater than the dealer's, but not more than 21.

THE DEAL

First draw cards to decide who is the dealer—the lowest card deals. Before the cards are dealt each player bets the amount he or she wants, but a maximum initial stake should be agreed beforehand. In diagram 1 each player has bet two chips. Then the dealer deals two cards faceup to each player and keeps two—one face up and the other face down.

Dealer

Player one

Player two

STAND, DOUBLE, HIT, OR SPLIT

At this point a player has different options (diagrams 1 and 2):

- To stand (or "stick")—that means to ask for no more cards from the dealer.
- To double the original stake but receive only one more card—a good bet if the cards total nine, ten, or 11. The chances of receiving a ten card are strong, which would give a good score to stand on.

- To hit (or "twist")—to be dealt an extra card faceup without increasing the stake. If a player's total goes above 21, they are "bust," and their stake goes to the dealer.
- If a player has a pair, they can "split" the cards and play each as a separate hand. They must bet an additional stake, the same as the original, to cover the second hand.
- If a player has an ace and a card worth ten, they have a "blackjack." If the dealer's upturned card shows that they do not have a blackjack, they must pay the player double their own stake. If the dealer also has a blackjack, neither side wins—the player's stake is returned.

1 *Here player one has 19 and decides to stand—the correct decision. Another card could make the total over 21. Player two has a blackjack. The dealer does not pay out yet since he or she might also have a blackjack. Player three's cards total 12. Three decides to hit and receives a 2, bringing the total to 14. Three hits again and gets a 10. The total is now 24, so three is bust. Player four has 11 and decides to double. Four receives one extra card, an 8—bringing the total to 19.*

Player three

Player four

Dealer

2 *At this point the dealer turns over their face down card—an 8. The dealer stands on this score of 18. It is time to settle up. Player one beat the dealer with 19. One wins four chips (two from the dealer plus their initial stake of two). Player two wins double their stake for a blackjack. Two gets six chips (four from the dealer plus their stake of two). Player three went bust and so loses their stake to the dealer. Player four doubled their initial stake to four and beat the dealer with 19. They win eight chips in total.*

Player one

Player two

Player three

Player four

1 *Poker hands are ranked in a set order from a royal flush (highest) to one pair (lowest). If players don't have either of these, the hand with the highest single card wins.*

Royal flush

Ace, king, queen, jack, and 10 of the same suit

Straight flush

Five cards of the same suit in rank order

Four of a kind

Four cards of the same rank

Full house

Three of a kind, plus a pair

Flush

Five cards of the same suit in any order

Straight

Five cards in rank order, regardless of suit

Three of a kind

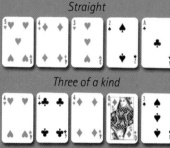

Three cards of the same rank

Two pairs

Two sets of two cards of the same rank

One pair

Two cards of the same rank

POKER

Poker is the favorite card game of the U.S. It is about bluffing, bravery, and cunning. Everyone has the chance to start with nothing and win a fortune through skill, luck, and perseverance.

DRAW POKER
There are several different poker games—Crazy Pineapple, London Lowball, Skinny Minnie, and Spit in the Ocean are only a few. The classic game of draw poker is the one played the most often. Five cards are dealt to between two and eight people, and then players bet on who has the best hand. Hands are ranked in a set order **(diagram 1)**.

SETTING UP
Before cards are dealt everyone pays an "ante"—an agreed starting bet—and also decides on the betting system. You can play "limit," in which bets are fixed—at two chips, for example. In "pot limit," you cannot bet more than the amount already in the pot. Or you can play "no limit," in which you can bet as many chips as you have on the table. The example hand in diagrams 2 and 3 shows pot limit.

Betting options

Check—to not make a bet. This is only possible if no bets have been made in that round.

Raise—to bet more than the previous player.

Call—to match the previous bet.

Call and raise—to match the previous bet and then increase the stakes again.

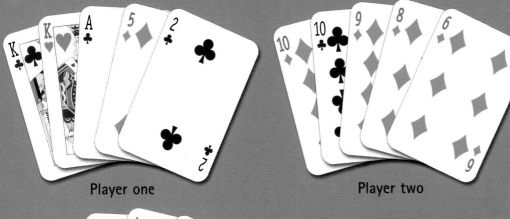

Player one

Player two

2 Here the three players have each paid an ante of one chip. Player one likes his or her pair of kings and raises one chip. Player two wants to continue in the hand, so he or she "calls." That means two matches player one's bet by adding one chip. Player three has two pairs thinks it is a good hand. Three calls by adding one chip and raises by six chips.

Players one and two must at least match player three's bet if they want to stay in the hand. They call by each adding six chips to the pot. All three players have now wagered the same amount (eight each), so the next phase of the game begins—the draw. Each player can now exchange any number of cards with the dealer. Player one trades three cards, player two trades one card, and player three also trades one card.

Player three

Pot

After the exchanges player one has not 3 improved his or her hand—still with a pair of kings, one checks. That means one does not bet anything but instead stays in the hand and keeps his or her options open. Player two has a flush. Two raises by ten chips. Player three has not improved on two pairs but is confident enough to stay in. Three calls, adding ten chips to match player two's bet. There are now 44 chips in the pot.

Returning to player one. To stay in the hand one has to add another ten chips. Is it worth it? Are the other two players bluffing? Not both of them! One decides not to take the risk and drops out.

The amount wagered by players two and three is now even, so the betting ends. It is time for the showdown. Player two wins the pot because two's flush beats player three's two pairs.

Player one

Player two

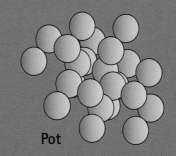

Pot

Player three

ANSWERS AND RESOURCES

GO TEST POSITION, PAGE 23

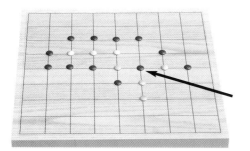

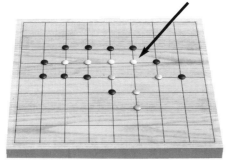

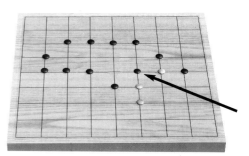

1 Black occupies the cutting point and threatens to capture four White stones.

2 White captures one Black stone, but Black has the final move . . .

3 Black plays a stone on to the eye in the middle of White's formation. The group of five White stones has been surrounded. They are removed from the board.

CHESS TEST POSITIONS, PAGE 29

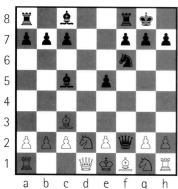

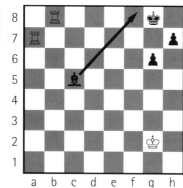

This is checkmate. White has lost the game.

This is not checkmate. Black can block the check from the rook by retreating the bishop to the f8 square.

MANCALA TEST POSITIONS, PAGE 33

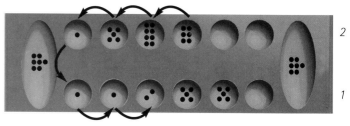

After sowing, player two will capture all the beans from the last three pots—seven in total.

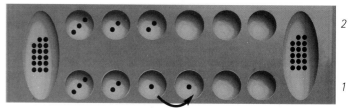

This simple move is the only way for player one to prevent player two from capturing any beans. The outcome of the game remains open.

CHECKERS TEST POSITIONS, PAGE 37

Starting position

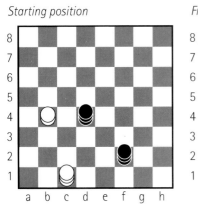

Final position

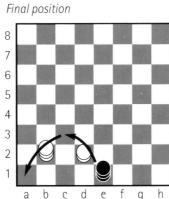

First Black moves from d4 to c3. White must capture—b4 to d2. Then Black blocks with f2 to e1. White only has one move—c1 to b2, after that Black captures both pieces. Black wins the game.

Starting position   *Final position*

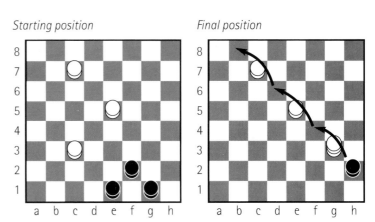

First Black gives away a piece—e1 to d2. White must capture, and in doing so gains a king—c3 to e1. Then Black gives away another piece—g1 to h2. White captures with e1 to g3. This perfectly lines up the pieces for Black to move in and take all of White's pieces—h2 to b8. Game over!

SPADES TEST HANDS, PAGE 53

It is too risky to make a nil bid. The king of spades could easily win a trick, and so could one of the clubs. There are no low cards in that suit to provide cover.

You could expect to win three tricks with this hand. Count one trick for the ace of hearts, one trick for either the king or queen of diamonds, and one trick for one of the four spade trumps.

THE INTERNET

There are several game web sites on the Internet where you can play most of the board and card games described in this book, in real time. Try the **www.yahoo.com** games site, or **www.zone.com** on MSN.

Many sites are dedicated to one particular game. These specialist sites often attract the real experts—and others, too! For example, the premier chess-playing web site is the Internet Chess Club at: **www.chessclub.com**. For backgammon try **www.gamesgrid.com**.

You can play an online version of the champion checkers program, Chinook, at **www.cs.ualberta.ca/~chinook/**. It's good practice before your next human opponent!

For a wide range of web sites about go, start off at the International Go Federation: **www.world-go.org**. From there you can find web sites that feature online games, tutorials, tests, tournament information, and contacts all over the world.

The best site for mancala is African Games: **www.myriadonline.com/awalink.htm**. Here you can find information on the game's history, the rules of different versions, where to play online—against humans and computers, and links to other web sites.

For card games the best place to start is at **www.pagat.com**. This site lists card games from all over the world and features rules, information, and links to other sites.

GLOSSARY

BOARD GAMES

BACKGAMMON

Anchor An important **point**, usually in the opponent's home board, occupied by two or more of your counters.

Back counters The two counters farthest from your **home board** at the start of the game.

Bar The central ridge between the two halves of the board. Captured counters are placed on the bar.

Bearing off Removing counters from the board at the end of the game. This can only happen if a player has brought all of his or her counters into the **home board**.

Blockade To restrict the movement of your opponent's counters by building **points**.

Blot A single, vulnerable piece.

Golden point (or **golden anchor**) The five point.

Hit To capture a piece.

Home board (or **inner board**) The quarter of the board where a player **bears off** his or her counters.

Outer board The area outside the home boards.

Point Any of the 24 spikes where the counters are placed. "Making a point" or "building a point" means moving two pieces on to the same spike. This makes them safe from attack.

Prime A row of four or more **points** that are each occupied by at least two counters—this forms a blockade.

Race A position where further **hits** are impossible, or very unlikely. The game's outcome depends on which player rolls the higher dice scores.

CHECKERS

Endgame A phase of the game in which both sides have made a **king**.

Jump (or **leap**) To make a capture.

King A single piece becomes a king when it reaches the final row of the board. A king is able to move backward and forward.

King row The final row of the board, where single pieces become **kings**.

CHESS

Castling A special move in which both the king and a rook can leave their starting squares on the same turn.

Check A piece that directly attacks the king is said to "give check" or put it "in check."

Checkmate The end of the game, when the king is put in **check** and cannot escape.

Diagonal A line of squares running obliquely across the board. Only the bishop and the queen are able to move along the diagonals.

Double check When two pieces put the **king** in **check** at the same time.

File The columns of squares that run up the board, marked by the letters "a" to "h."

Major piece A queen or a rook.

Minor piece A knight or a bishop.

Promotion When a pawn reaches the eighth rank and turns into a knight, a bishop, a rook, or a queen. Because the queen is so powerful other pieces are rarely selected.

Rank The rows of squares that run across the board, marked by the numbers 1 to 8.

Resignation When a player gives up the game before checkmate occurs, knowing that defeat is inevitable.

Stalemate When a player cannot make any legal moves but is not in check. The game ends as a tie.

GO

Atari When stones are threatened with capture, they are said to be in "atari."

Cutting point A point that, if occupied, could divide and weaken an opponent's **group** of stones.

Eye An unoccupied point in the middle of a **group** of stones.

Group Two or more stones belonging to one player in the same area. It is often difficult to say whether a group is weak or strong. A group that has two **eyes** is safe from capture.

Intersection The point where two lines cross. Stones are placed on these points.

Komi Points (usually five and a half) added to White's score as compensation for Black having the first move. This is an optional rule.

Liberty An unoccupied point directly next to a stone, horizontally or vertically.

Wei-chi The Chinese word for go.

MANCALA

Sowing beans Moving pieces around the board.

Store hole Where captured beans are placed.

CARD GAMES

Ace high When the ace ranks as the highest card in a suit.

Ace low When the ace ranks as the lowest card in a suit.

Chip A game token.

Court card (or face card) A king, queen, or jack.

Cut To place the lower half of the pack on top of the upper half.

Deal To distribute cards to the players.

Deck A pack of cards.

Lead To play the first card.

Lead, the The first card played.

Turn-up card The top card of a pack, turned faceup and placed either on top of the pack or next to it.

BLACKJACK

Blackjack Two cards that total 21—an ace plus a ten or a court card.

Bust When a player's cards total more than 21, he or she is bust and loses their stake.

Double To double the original stake but receive just one more card—a good option if the two original cards total nine, ten, or eleven.

Hit (or twist) To receive another card from the dealer.

Push A tie between dealer and player. The player takes back the original stake.

Split If you are dealt a pair, the cards can be split and played as two separate hands.

Stand (or stick) To decline to take another card from the dealer.

CRIBBAGE

Crib (or box) The hand of four cards formed by the discards of the players.

Flush Four or five cards that are all of the same suit.

Game hole The 121st hole on the cribbage board—the end of the game.

Go Said by a player when he or she cannot lay a card without the running total exceeding 31 points.

Run (or sequence) Three or more cards in rank order. The cards do not have to be of the same suit.

Show, the When the players take back their own cards and announce scoring combinations.

"Ten" cards The kings, queens, jacks, and tens.

Thirty-one (31) When the running total of the cards played hits exactly 31, the player scores two points.

HEARTS

Break hearts To discard the first heart as a penalty point. Until a heart has been discarded, the heart suit cannot be **led**.

Shoot the moon To win all the penalty points.

POKER

Ante A compulsory bet placed by all the players before the deal.

Bluff To bet or raise with a bad hand in the hope that the other players will be scared off and **fold**.

Fold To throw in your hand.

Pot, the The total amount bet by the players.

Showdown The display of cards at the end of the hand.

RUMMY

Discard pile A pile made up of cards dumped by the players.

Lay off To add an individual card to an existing **meld**.

Meld A set of three or more cards—either three or four of a kind, or a **run** of at least three cards.

Run (or sequence) Three or more cards in rank order, all of the same suit.

Stock or stock pile The pile of undealt cards.

SPADES

Bid The declared number of **tricks** that a player expects to make.

Blind nil A nil bid declared before looking at the cards.

Break spades To lay the first spade as a **trump** card. Spades cannot be **led** until this happens.

Contract The number of **tricks** that a **partnership** aims to make.

Nil bid A player who makes a nil bid must avoid taking any **tricks**.

Overtricks **Tricks** made above the stated bid.

Sandbags (or bags) Penalty points for **overtricks**. For every ten sandbags, 100 points is deducted from a **partnership's** score.

WHIST

Partnership Players sitting opposite who play together.

Revoke To fail to follow suit when able to do so—this incurs a penalty.

Trick A round of cards, one from each player.

Trump To lay a trump card on a plain suit.

Trumps A superior suit. A card from the trump suit beats any card from another suit.

Void Having no cards in a suit.

INDEX